THE EARTH STRIKES BACK

HOW WE USE AND ABUSE OUR PLANET

WATER

Pamela Grant and Arthur Haswell

Thameside Press

U.S. publication copyright © 2000 Thameside Press.
International copyright reserved in all countries.
No part of this book may be reproduced in any form
without written permission from the publisher.

Distributed in the United States by
Smart Apple Media
1980 Lookout Drive
North Mankato, MN56003

Copyright © Belitha Press Limited 2000
Text copyright © Pamela Grant and Arthur Haswell
2000

Series editor Mary-Jane Wilkins
Editor Susie Brooks
Designer Helen James
Picture researcher Diana Morris
Illustrator William Donohoe
Consultant Chris Baines

Printed in China

9 8 7 6 5 4 3 2 1

Library of Congress Cataloging-in-Publication Data
Grant, Pamela
   Water / by Pamela Grant & Arthur Haswell.
   p.cm.—(Earth strikes back)
   Includes index.
   Summary: Examines major environmental issues
surrounding water, giving examples of attempts to
solve global problems and sources for more
information.
   ISBN 1-929298-60-9
   1. Water—Juvenile literature. 2. Water—
Pollution—Juvenile literature. 3. Aquatic ecology—
Juvenile literature. [1. Water. 2. Water—Pollution.
3. Pollution. 4. Aquatic ecology. 5. Ecology.]
I. Haswell, Arthur. II. Title. III. Series.

   GB662.3.G73 2000
   333.91—dc21
                              00-024937

Words in **bold** are explained in the glossary on
pages 46 and 47.

Contents

Water world

Seen from space, the Earth looks blue and white because of its oceans, ice caps, and clouds. Water helps make Earth different from other planets.

In the beginning

All life around us needs water to survive. But there hasn't always been water on Earth. About 4,500 million years ago, when this planet was new, it was a huge spinning mass of hot, molten rock—without rivers and seas. Gradually, the rock cooled and became solid. As it cooled, gases and **water vapor** were given off. These made up the **atmosphere**.

Starting life

The first rain fell about 3,850 million years ago, as water vapor in the atmosphere cooled. This rain spread over newly-hardened rocks, forming the oceans and seas. Deep under the oceans are hot pockets of gas where **bacteria** thrive. Similar bacteria were probably the first-ever forms of life.

▼ *Water is home to millions of life forms. The sea off Papua New Guinea is alive with plants, fish, and other marine creatures.*

◀ The blue area on this picture of Earth is the vast Pacific Ocean. The ice caps of the Arctic and Antarctic look white.

Sculpting the land

For 2,750 million years, all Earth's life was in water. Plants and animals only began to live on land about 500 million years ago. And land itself was shaped by water. Deep under the oceans, volcanoes erupted, creating islands. Rain washing down slopes carved out valleys and made rivers. Loose stones and sand, carried by the water's flow, built up in layers to form **sedimentary rock**. Water is still sculpting land in this way today.

Patterns of change

For thousands of years humans, like animals and plants, used water without disturbing nature's balance too much. And some people still live in this way. But during the last two centuries industries, transport, and populations have grown so fast that they have affected the Earth's water.

Water on Earth is changing. Drought now leaves more and more areas dry, while elsewhere land is swamped by uncontrollable floods. Across the world, life in rivers, lakes, and seas is being destroyed as humans cause harmful **pollution**.

▶ The rushing water of the Nooksack River cuts a path through the woods of Baker National Park, Washington.

Making peace with our planet

We each affect our planet just by living. A single person may not change things much, but large groups can overwhelm and destroy natural systems. As world populations grow and technology gives us more power, we must work to repair damage by humans, and live in harmony with our environment.

Water and us

Water is truly amazing. It's not alive, and we do not make it, yet we cannot survive without it. We use water in many different ways to make our lives easier.

Water for life

The food we eat contains water, and so do we. If all the water in our bodies was removed we would shrivel, in the way that a grape dries, becoming a raisin. We each need to take in about 4 pints of water every day. Although we may be able to survive for about three weeks without food, we could not go without a drink for much more than four days. All creatures on Earth depend on water to stay alive.

▲ *We should each drink about eight glasses of water a day to stay healthy. We get some water from the food we eat.*

▼ *In all, more than 26,700 gallons of water may be used when making a car.*

Water for industry

The manufacture of almost every item you can buy requires water—from paper to shoes, to the plastic bags around them. A complicated item, such as a car, is made up of thousands of parts, all of which need water to be produced.

Not surprisingly, many factories are built next to rivers or lakes. This allows their final products to be taken away by ship. Transport along rivers, and across lakes and oceans, is often the cheapest way of moving things in bulk.

Water at home

In richer countries, most people have access to water whenever they want it, simply by turning on a faucet. Pipes in most homes supply baths, showers, washing machines, and toilets. Hoses allow people to water their gardens and wash their cars.

Water for leisure

Water also plays a vital part away from our homes. People use it for leisure activities, such as swimming and water sports. It may keep us cool in hot weather. Water can also enable people to travel from place to place, by slow ship or fast Hovercraft.

▼ *Merchant ships carry more than 560 million tons of cargo over the world's seas every year.*

Water for all?

Not everyone on Earth uses the same amount of water. Though people in richer countries are used to a constant supply, more than half the world's population still lives without a faucet in their own home. In the U.S., every person uses an average of 134 gallons of water every day, but in Central African countries such as Uganda, people often make do with less than 2 gallons each.

Water for power

Electricity is also dependent on water. **Hydroelectricity** stations use its flow to generate energy. Other power stations convert water to steam to drive **turbines**.

Water's ways

Water exists on Earth in three forms—as a gas called water vapor, as a liquid, or frozen as ice. It is always changing, according to its environment.

The water cycle

Water is constantly **evaporating** from the surface of oceans, lakes, and rivers. The water vapor given off forms clouds that can be blown along by the wind. When clouds cool, their vapor **condenses** and falls as rain— back into the sea, or onto land where it collects in streams. These streams feed lakes, and join together to form rivers that flow back to the sea.

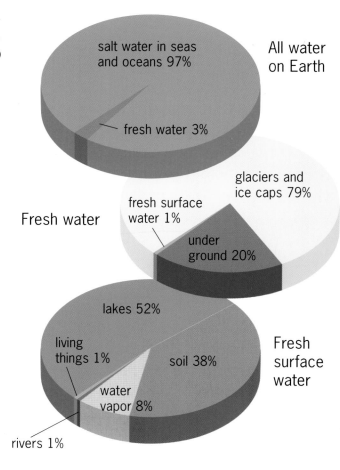

All water on Earth

salt water in seas and oceans 97%

fresh water 3%

Fresh water

fresh surface water 1%

glaciers and ice caps 79%

under ground 20%

Fresh surface water

lakes 52%

living things 1%

soil 38%

water vapor 8%

rivers 1%

▲ Only three percent of the Earth's water is the fresh water needed for land life.

▼ Water moves around and changes state in the water cycle.

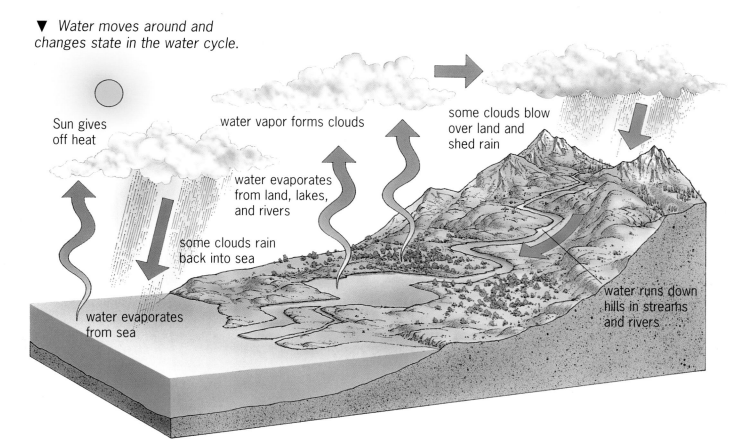

Sun gives off heat

water vapor forms clouds

some clouds blow over land and shed rain

water evaporates from land, lakes, and rivers

some clouds rain back into sea

water evaporates from sea

water runs down hills in streams and rivers

Water, water everywhere

Water covers 70 percent of the Earth. The sea's salt water makes up 97 percent of this. Most of the rest is frozen as ice, around the Poles or in **glaciers**. Some is locked in **aquifers** deep under the ground. Only one percent is fresh surface water, essential for land life. This exists in lakes, rivers, soil, and living things, and as vapor in the air.

Relying on rainfall

Rain is one of our main sources of fresh water. But it doesn't fall evenly over the world—or over time. While some areas have regular wet and dry seasons, many receive little or no rain all year round. Others suffer sudden downpours and floods. Rainwater must be conserved and distributed carefully if it is to benefit everyone.

▼ *The dense vegetation of this tropical rain forest generates its own clouds.*

Enough to go around?

There is so much water on Earth that there should be enough for everyone. But people are now taking almost twice as much water from rivers, lakes, and aquifers as they did 40 years ago. And humans are polluting water with harmful waste and chemicals. We all need clean, fresh water to survive, but many areas of the world are now suffering as supplies run out.

Nature's stores

Plants collect water through their roots, and give it out again as vapor through their leaves. Rain forests, with their vast crowds of trees, even produce their own clouds. Forests and **wetlands** are some of nature's water stores. Looking after water also means looking after these areas.

Passing poisons

Water is always on the move around the water cycle, along rivers and across the oceans. Much can be carried in its flow—including pollution.

Finding flavor

Water has no flavor or smell. The saltiness of the sea is the taste of chemicals **dissolved** from rocks. Any pollution adds its own flavor and smell to the water it enters.

Water's web of life

Tiny plants and animals called **plankton** are the basis of ocean life. Shrimp-like creatures feed on them, and are themselves eaten by small fish. Bigger fish eat them, and birds, animals, and people complete the **food chain** by eating the bigger fish.

▲ *A drop of ocean water like this may contain hundreds of microscopic plankton.*

Poisons humans dump into the water are taken in by plankton, which pass them onto fish that eat them, and so on along the food chain. By the time we eat them ourselves, these poisons may have built up to harmful levels.

Washing up waste

Pollution from water can also be washed up onto the land. For example, a river that has been polluted by chemicals from a factory or farm will spread some of those poisons along its banks. Tides wash up pollution from the sea onto beaches and cliffs, even if the waste has been dumped far from the shore.

◄ *When a big fish eats a smaller fish, it takes in anything the small fish has in its body. Poisons pass up the food chain in this way.*

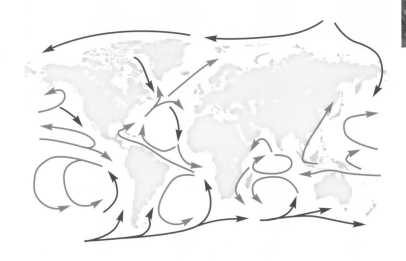

▶ *Water circles around the oceans in currents. The red lines on this map are warm currents, the blue lines are cold.*

Water on the move

Water can travel vast distances. The oceans have a system of **currents**—huge circuits of warm or cold water, blown by different winds. Currents can carry water over thousands of miles. Pollutants, such as oil released from a ship or trash thrown overboard, move around the world with these currents.

Pollution can be spread in other ways by the **water cycle**. Not only is it carried by the flow of rivers and seas, but also by clouds. Any chemicals dissolved in the water vapor may be blown a long way before they fall as **acid rain**.

▼ *Humans are at the top of the food chain, so by polluting water, we may be poisoning ourselves.*

Keep it clean

Water pollution is everyone's problem. When **sewage**, chemicals from farming and industry, oil, and nuclear waste enter the water cycle, fish, animals, and plants are all affected—and so are we. Dirty water is harmful and unpleasant. Around the world, people are realizing the benefits of keeping water clean. We need to work together to prevent any further pollution.

Finding fresh water

Early towns were built beside rivers, lakes, or wells which supplied water. But growing populations and increasing technology have brought more demand for fresh water, and new ways of collecting it.

Piping water

The city of Rome developed beside the River Tiber over 2,500 years ago. As the city grew, extra water had to be brought in from nearby hills. The Romans built **aqueducts** to do this. New York, situated beside the mouth of the Hudson River, has the same system today. In the 1860s, it became the first modern city to pipe in fresh water.

▲ The Wemmershoek dam keeps water in this reservoir at a water treatment plant on the Cape Peninsula, South Africa.

▼ Roman aqueducts were almost level, so water moved along them slowly. This one crosses the River Gardon in France.

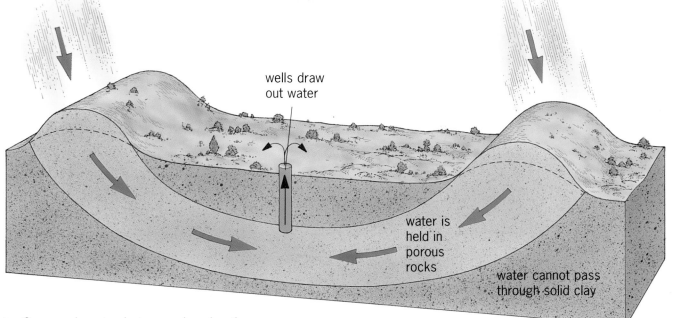

wells draw out water

water is held in porous rocks

water cannot pass through solid clay

▲ *Some rainwater is trapped under the ground in aquifers. It can be reached by drilling down into the porous rock.*

Man-made lakes

Reservoirs are a modern way of collecting and storing fresh water, ready to be piped to towns and cities or used to produce electricity. These man-made lakes are usually created by building **dams** across rivers to contain the flow of water.

Underground supplies

Most of the Earth's fresh water is locked in **porous** rock deep under the ground. Many areas depend on these sources—known as aquifers—particularly where the climate is hot and dry. A well is a hole that is dug or drilled into the water-laden rock. Modern pumping stations draw vast quantities of water out of aquifers.

Carrying the load

Many parts of the world today do not have adequate water-collecting systems. Some have used up local water supplies and cannot afford the technology to bring in water from elsewhere. In poorer countries, many people still have to walk for long distances to collect water. To transport it home, they may fill jars or buckets and carry these on their heads.

► *Modern pumping stations, such as this one in London, England, draw huge amounts of water from aquifers.*

Cleaning up

Rivers, lakes, and reservoirs are often unclean. Water must be purified to make it safe to use—and any waste needs to be treated before the water is returned to its natural source.

▲ *This untreated sewage is flowing into a river in France, causing pollution.*

Pure water

In richer countries today, water is usually cleaned and purified at a water treatment works. Here the solid waste is removed, and small dissolved particles are left to settle before being carefully filtered out. Chemicals, such as **chlorine**, are then added to the water to destroy any germs. Finally, the clean water is pumped through pipes to our homes, schools, farms, and factories.

Down the drain

Used water is flushed down drains and toilets every day. This human waste, or sewage, contains harmful germs. If water is returned to a river, lake, or sea in this state, it damages plants, fish, and local wildlife.

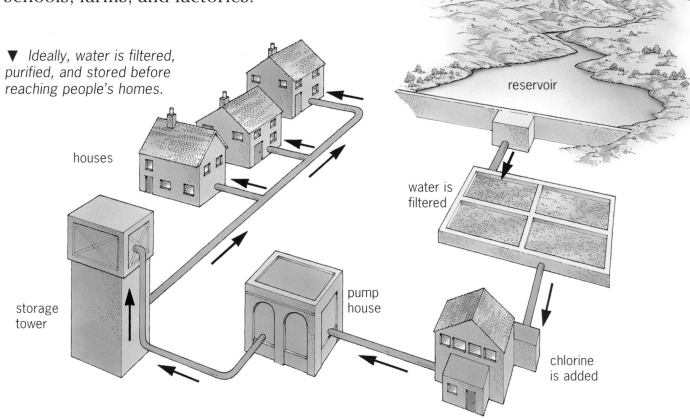

▼ *Ideally, water is filtered, purified, and stored before reaching people's homes.*

houses

storage tower

pump house

reservoir

water is filtered

chlorine is added

Sifting sewage

Raw sewage is still being released, with devastating effect, into rivers, lakes, and seas all over the world. But in richer countries, most human waste is now carried down pipes to a **sewer**, which should lead to a sewage treatment plant.

Here, large objects are separated out first, as at a water treatment works. Then the water is pumped into huge tanks, where the smaller solids are left to settle. They form a thick sewage sludge, which can be taken away and used as a fertilizer to help crops grow.

The rest of the liquid sewage passes through a series of **filter beds**—open pits filled with coarse gravel. **Microorganisms** among the stones break down the waste, cleaning the water. Then it is piped back into a river, lake, or sea.

▼ *Beckton Sewage Works, London, England, processes waste from two million people.*

Living Machines

In the natural world, small amounts of dirty water can be cleaned by plants and animals. A system called the Living Machine uses this process to treat larger quantities of sewage and industrial waste without using chemicals. Waste water passes through a series of tanks filled with algae, plants, fish, snails, and other living creatures. These eat away at the waste, cleaning the water until it is ready to be returned to the sea. Europe's first Living Machine began work in 1995 at the Findhorn Foundation, Scotland.

Good enough to drink?

When we turn on a faucet, we expect clean fresh water to come out. But for many people, this is still a luxury. Drinking or washing in dirty water can be very unhealthy.

The Great Stink

In the 1800s, the River Thames in London, England, became an open sewer as new flush toilets filled it with untreated waste. Disease spread, killing thousands, including Queen Victoria's husband, Prince Albert. People named 1858 the Year of the Great Stink because of the stench. Parliament decided to act, and by 1861 the first pipes were laid to carry sewage out of London.

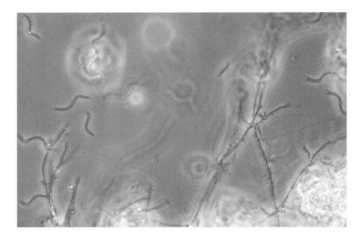

▲ *Microscopic bugs in sewage can cause deadly diseases if they enter water supplies.*

Killer bugs

The diseases that struck Victorian London were **cholera** and **typhoid**. They are caused by microscopic bacteria in dirty water, and are still common in poorer parts of the world. In these areas, some people may drink from the same water they wash in or use as a toilet.

▼ *Work on London's first sewers was under way by 1862, when this photo was taken.*

◄ *This girl in Nepal is washing her dishes in dirty street water. Every day, about 25,000 people die as a result of using unclean water. Most of these victims are children.*

The plague

In Europe centuries ago, filth and poor sanitation attracted swarms of rats, which caused deadly outbreaks of **plague**. In September 1994, floods washed dead animals, human waste, and rubbish onto the streets of Surat, India. Rats spread plague again, and many people fled their homes. But a massive clean-up soon controlled the outbreak. Now Surat is India's second cleanest city.

Deadly diarrhea

About 80 percent of all illness in the world is caused by dirty water. Drinking it can give you diarrhea. An upset stomach like this may not seem serious to us, but diarrhea is the biggest killer of children in the world. One in ten babies born in parts of Africa, Asia, and South America die from it.

Wicked worms

In many hot countries, disease is also spread by **parasites** living in dirty water. In Africa, Asia, and South America, for example, hookworms burrow through the skin of people's feet, damaging their bodies and even killing them. Harmful roundworms and guinea worms are also common.

Piping fresh water

The people of Hitosa, Ethiopia, once had to walk up to 30 miles to find water. But now a new system brings it to their towns and villages from two natural **springs**. Backed by the charity Wateraid, local people helped to raise money and lay 88 miles of pipes. Many villagers have been trained so that now more than 60,000 people in Hitosa can have clean, fresh water.

Drying up

Freshwater sources depend on rain for topping up—but we often use more water than nature can replace. If we take too much, rivers, lakes, wells, and reservoirs will dry up.

▲ *Farms with wheat fields, such as this one in Nebraska, use huge amounts of water. This can drain aquifers dry.*

Great American desert

The Ogallala Aquifer is 750 miles long and runs from Nebraska to Texas. It once seemed an inexhaustible supply, and farms grew up around 150,000 wells. But for each gallon of water pumped out, only about a cupful is replaced by rainfall. Many wells are now running dry as the level of the **water table** falls. Farmers are unable to water their crops and their fields are turning to dust.

Running aground

The Panama Canal is a man-made waterway, cutting into 51 miles of countryside between the Pacific and Atlantic Oceans. At each end, three **locks** raise and lower ships by 435 feet. Every ship that sails out of the last lock into the ocean takes 53 million gallons of water with it.

The canal's water is provided by rivers which become torrents in the rainy season. Reservoirs collect flood water to feed the canal throughout the year. But during 1997 and 1998, the rains failed. Reservoirs emptied and the water level in the canal fell. In order to float higher in the water, ships had to travel with lighter cargo, making their trips less worthwhile.

◄ *Locks in the Panama Canal, allow ships to sail upstream between hills.*

▲ The fairy-tale scenery of France's Loire Valley is threatened as too much water is taken from the river and levels begin to fall.

Lowering levels

The River Loire in France flows between banks of vineyards and towns topped with castles. Both grapes and people need water, and so much has been taken from the river that now its level has fallen. This is threatening local wetlands and marshes and destroying the area's natural beauty.

Proposals to build two dams along the River Loire would have destroyed countryside, and led to even less water flowing along the river. But during the 1990s, local people and **environmentalists** got together and campaigned against the dams, until eventually the plans were abandoned.

Sharing water

The Nebraska Groundwater Foundation is working to save the Ogallala Aquifer. It holds an annual children's festival which attracts thousands. The message is that enough rain falls for everyone, as long as water is used sparingly and people cooperate. Some communities on the Great Plains are doing just that. Towns that used to pump from their own wells now take water from farms, and then return the treated waste water for the crops.

Chemicals flowing

Industries which use water are often built beside rivers or near the coast. Water is pumped into the factories, and returned after use. But pollutants may be added in the process, making the water poisonous.

Harmful heavy metal

The Japanese love eating fish, and the people of Minamata have their own fleet of fishing boats—but in the 1950s a strange illness overtook the town. People couldn't talk properly, and their hands and feet felt numb. Eventually 2,000 became ill and 400 died. They had been poisoned by mercury, which had collected in the fish they were catching. The mercury had come from a local factory. It is a common **heavy metal** pollutant, along with lead and arsenic.

Deadly digging

Under the ground at Grasberg, Indonesia, there are over 2.2 billion tonnes of copper ore. In digging it out, mining companies pump 137,500 tons of waste into local rivers every day, killing the fish and nearby sago trees.

Local people, such as the Kamoro tribe, live off fish and sago. If they are to continue their way of life, the mining pollution must stop. But the government of Indonesia wants the money the mines make, and uses its army to stop people protesting.

In August and September 1997, nine tribal people were killed in suspicious circumstances. As the mine continues to expand today, protected by 6,000 soldiers, the local environment remains under constant threat.

◄ *This river is filled with pollution from the Grasberg copper mine in West Papua, Indonesia.*

▲ *A new treatment works at the BASF factory, near Ludwigshafen, Germany, removes chemicals from used water before it is pumped back into the Rhine.*

Cleaning up the Rhine

The River Rhine in Europe flows through land that is scattered with factories. Between 1920 and 1970, the quantity of heavy metals and chemicals released in the area rose by over 400 percent.

But worries about pollution brought a change of attitude, and new laws were passed. Polluting companies were fined, and this led to the development of new cleaning techniques.

The BASF chemical factory on the River Rhine in Germany is the largest of its kind in Europe. New treatment works and filters now ensure that chemicals and heavy metals are removed from the water it pumps back into the river.

Keeping the lid on

The Alsek River (below) flows through a wilderness in Canada. There are no roads, and the local bears and eagles have the place to themselves. When a mining company found gold, silver, and copper there, it planned to cut the top off a nearby mountain to reach the ore, threatening the river with waste from the mine. But public protest forced the state authorities to make all mining there illegal. They turned the area into a wilderness park, saving it for the bears and eagles, and the salmon in the rivers.

It's raining acid

Cars, factories, and coal-burning power stations fill the air with smoke. Chemicals in this smoke mix with the water vapor in clouds. When rain falls from polluted clouds, it can cause widespread damage.

Acid attack

Rain polluted by chemicals in smoke (such as **hydrocarbons**, sulfur, and nitrogen) is called acid rain. It makes plants become feeble and die, harms wildlife, and eats away at stonework. In Germany, so many trees have been killed by acid rain that people have invented a new word—*waldsterben*—which means "the death of forests."

Lifeless lakes

Over the last 70 years, acid has built up in lakes in the Adirondack Mountains. Once famous for ospreys, otters, and trout, many of the lakes are now lifeless. Plants and fish were killed by the acid, and animals and birds which fed on them have gone.

▼ *Trees in the Erzgbeirge Mountains, between Germany and Czechoslovakia, have been badly damaged by acid rain.*

Beating acid

Once acid rain stops falling, damaged forests soon revive—and as a lake becomes less acidic, water life returns. People from around the world have met to work out how to reduce acid rain. Power stations are switching to low-sulfur coal and attempting to clean up their smoke. New cars are being fitted with **catalytic converters** and major polluters have been fined. Each country needs to find its own way of reducing toxic fumes.

▲ *Chemical factories in Shanghai, China, puff out clouds of smoke, polluting the air and causing acid rain.*

▼ *Fumes from cars and cities contribute to acid rain. These smoke-filled clouds hang over Los Angeles.*

Getting together

Industries in China produce some of the world's worst air pollution —and they don't damage only their local plants and wildlife. Clouds carrying chemicals from China are spreading acid rain to Japan. The Japanese say that their lakes will be lifeless in 30 years if this continues. Now the Japanese are helping the Chinese to clean up their smoke. When affected countries get together like this, the threat to water, plants, and people begins to lessen.

Green hair

When acid rain enters our water supplies, the chemicals can dissolve metal pipes. Where pipes are made of copper, this can turn baths, sinks, and even your hair green. Drinking the water could give you diarrhea.

Sea pollution

Millions of tons of waste find their way into the world's oceans every year. From litter dropped on beaches to oil spilled by ships, there are many causes of sea pollution—and the effects can be devastating.

▲ Many nuclear power stations are situated near the sea. This is Torness in East Lothian, Scotland.

Black death

Every year nearly 4 million tons of oil spills into the sea. Most of this comes from ships. When oil is spilled, some of it sinks, poisoning fish and plants. The rest floats, spreading to form vast slicks that cut off **oxygen** from the water. The feathers of birds landing in the oil become matted, so they can no longer keep out the cold.

When the oil tanker *Sea Empress* hit rocks off South Wales in 1996, nearly 67,000 tons of oil spread over 156 miles of coastline, killing 50,000 birds. This ship had a single hull. New tankers have two hulls, one inside the other. When the double-hulled *Borga* hit the same rocks that year, no oil was spilled.

▼ People clean up the damage from an oil slick washed onto a beach in Wales.

The invisible killer

Waste from nuclear power stations is **radioactive** and poisonous, and it stays that way for thousands of years. No one wants it dumped near them, so the sea seems the obvious place. But this harms fish and makes them dangerous to eat. Sea dumping was banned in the U.S. in 1970, and in Europe in 1982. But five years later a beach near the Sellafield Nuclear Plant, England was found to be 1,000 times more radioactive than normal.

▲ *Before being banned in 1998, nearly a quarter of England's sewage sludge was dumped at sea by ships such as this one.*

Blue flag beaches

Coasts can become polluted with oil, sewage, or garbage, and beaches can be badly affected with filthy water. In Europe, all beaches and tourist resorts are now tested regularly. Only those that pass all 26 criteria—including having clean water and well-managed, safe beaches—can fly the blue flag. A leaflet published every year lists all the Blue Flag beaches, so anyone looking for clean fun beside the sea knows where to go.

The sea is our toilet

All over the world sewage is pumped untreated into the sea, or carried in ships and dumped. The Mid-Atlantic Bight, an area of sea 100 miles from New York, receives around 8.8 million tons of raw sewage every year. Sea urchins there have 25 percent sewage sludge in their bodies.

Seas that are surrounded by land probably suffer the most. Countries by the Mediterranean Sea all pollute it with their waste—but because the sea is not owned by any one of them, people don't want to spend money on cleaning it. In 1998, the **European Union** banned sewage dumping. People need to work together in the future to keep the sea clean.

Threats from farming

Modern farmers spray their crops with chemicals to make them grow bigger and to kill pests, helping them to produce more food. But what happens to these chemicals after they have done their job?

Silent spring

In 1962, fish and birds living around a small American town began to die, until the sky and rivers were empty. The killer was a **pesticide** called DDT, sprayed on fields to poison insects which fed on the crops. But birds ate the insects, and rain washed the DDT into soil and rivers. Plants and fish took it in. Animals and birds ate the plants and fish, and so the chemicals passed along the food chain.

The more the creatures ate, the more DDT collected in their bodies, until at last they died. DDT was eventually banned in America and Western Europe. But factories kept making it, and sent it to poorer countries. In some of these places it is still used today.

▼ *Crop-spraying on modern farms can pollute ground water and nearby rivers with harmful chemicals.*

▲ *Where nitrates build up in water, an algal bloom can spread thickly. This mass of algae has built up over a lake in Sweden.*

Nasty nitrates

Nitrates are chemicals produced naturally by the soil, and are needed for plant growth. Where land is used to grow crops year after year, the level of nitrates drops. Farmers have always spread animal manure to remedy this. Over the last 100 years, **artificial fertilizers** have been used increasingly, but these can build up nitrates to harmful levels.

Excess nitrates can seep down into ground water, making it dangerous to drink. They also run into streams and rivers, lakes, and seas. As levels build up in the water, they can harm plants and animals. But certain plant forms, called algae, thrive on nitrates. These can spread over the water's surface.

In the past, farmers treated their soil with rotted manure to supply nitrates, and grew their crops without artificial chemicals. Some fruit and vegetables suffered from pests and diseases, but enough thrived to be sold at a profit, and people didn't expect to produce perfect crops. Today's organic farmers rely on old methods. Their food is free from pesticides and other chemicals. Organic food is generally tastier, healthier, and less damaging to the environment than non-organic food—but it costs more to buy.

Blooming water

Algae cut off the light and oxygen that plants and fish need to survive. They gradually destroy water life by forming a blanket called **algal bloom**. Off the northeast coast of the U.S., an algal bloom known as The Dead Zone forms every summer as fertilizers spread on fields many miles away drain into the ocean water.

Watering the land

Where there is not enough rainfall to grow food, water can be brought to dry land along aqueducts, canals, ditches, or pipes. This is called irrigation. But irrigation uses up lots of water and can drain rivers and lakes dry.

Flooding fields

Rice is the staple diet in many hot countries, and huge amounts of water are needed to grow it. Paddy fields (*paddy* means rice) must be flooded before planting. Water is held in the fields by a series of low banks. When the rice has ripened, the fields are drained before harvesting begins.

Many rice-growing areas rely on the heavy rains of the **monsoon** season to flood their paddy fields. If this water is properly stored, it can then be channeled to the fields to grow crops at drier times of the year.

▼ *The terraced banks of paddy fields hold all the water needed for rice planting.*

A shrinking sea

In areas where there is not enough rain, the results of **irrigation** can be devastating. The Aral Sea in West Asia used to be the fourth largest lake in the world. But now it is drying up. Rivers that feed the Aral Sea have been drained to irrigate cotton fields, and water levels have dropped. Boats that once bobbed on the waves of the lake are now stranded on dry land.

▲ Desert plants now grow in the hulls of boats stranded in the dried-up Aral Sea.

Draining rivers dry

Californian farmers grow vegetables on very dry land. Irrigation systems there even water fields in the middle of the desert. But these have helped to drain rivers and aquifers dry. So much water has been piped from the mighty Colorado River that now only a muddy trickle flows into the sea.

Salt in the soil

In hot countries, water evaporates very quickly. When land has been irrigated, evaporation leaves behind **minerals** and salts. These build up in the soil, making the ground less **fertile**. Irrigated fields in Pakistan produce much less food than they used to because of this problem. Eventually soil may become infertile, and farmers will have to move away.

▼ Fields of crops can be grown in the desert with the help of modern irrigation.

Food from the sea

Irrigation may not be the only way of farming dry land. Instead we could grow plants that need very little water or that survive in difficult soils. One kind of garden beet, for example, can grow in water that is three-quarters seawater. We can also learn from native ways of growing food. The Aborigines harvest wild plants in the dry lands of Australia, while the Seri Indians of Mexico grind flour from eelgrass taken from the sea.

To dam or not to dam?

Damming rivers is one way of storing water to provide cities and farms with a constant supply—this also generates electricity. But building dams is expensive and may take many years. Dams also affect the land that surrounds them.

Drowned worlds

Since ancient times, people living by the River Nile in Egypt have relied on yearly floods to water their fields. In the 1960s, the High Aswan Dam was built to store flood water and provide irrigation all year round. But as building went on, the dam's reservoir threatened to flood Ancient Egyptian sites, including the temples of Abu Simbel. In a race against time, the temples had to be moved to higher ground to save them.

▲ The Hoover Dam, Arizona/Nevada, is one of the largest dams in the world. Its reservoir, Lake Mead, is popular for sailing and windsurfing.

Increased earthquakes

The Colorado River has 19 dams that provide water for farms and cities many miles away. The Hoover Dam can hold two years' river flow in its reservoir, Lake Mead. But when the lake was first built, people noticed an increase in small earthquakes in the area. The water's weight could be to blame. It is making the ground under the lake sink by about half-an-inch each year.

◄ The temples of Abu Simbel were cut into more than 1,000 blocks, which were moved to higher ground and put back together again.

The Three Gorges

The Three Gorges Dam is China's biggest engineering project since the Great Wall. The dam will help stop flooding on the Yangtze River, which has killed many thousands of people over the years. It will also house the world's most productive hydroelectric plant, which could enable China to close many of its coal-fired power stations that belch out smoke, causing acid rain.

But a new reservoir behind the dam will drown 150,000 acres of land, including 160 towns, and 1.3 million local people are having to move away from their homes. Three unspoilt gorges, where the Yangtze flows between cliffs, will also disappear under the water.

People's protest

In 1991, the government of India planned to build 2,000 dams along the River Narmada, threatening to destroy towns and villages along its banks. At Sardar-Sarovar, the site of the largest dam, people formed a protest group called the "Save or Drown Squad." They said they would rather be drowned than move from their homes. Eventually, an Indian court ordered work on the dam to be stopped. Other dams were also abandoned after people protested.

▼ *The pale blue shading shows the area that will be flooded when the Three Gorges Dam is completed.*

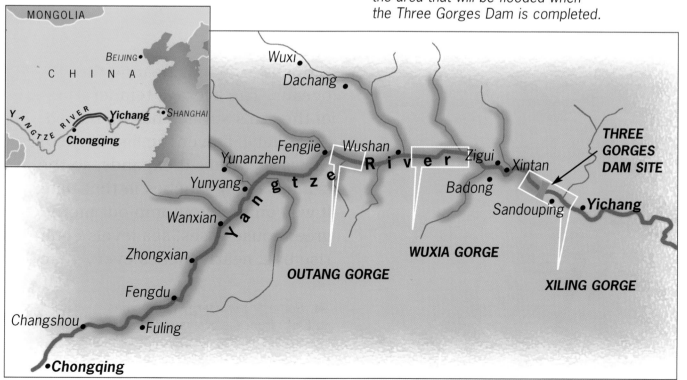

Climate change

The Earth's weather has never been constant. It was once so cold that ice covered half of North America and Europe. Now the world's climate is becoming hotter and drier. This is partly linked to our increasing pollution of the air.

In the greenhouse

Some of the Sun's energy, which lights and warms us, is reflected back from the Earth. As it passes through the atmosphere, some gases absorb it and give off heat. These are the **greenhouse gases**. The more they build up in the air, the more heat they give out, and the hotter the Earth becomes. This is called **global warming**.

Pollution accelerates global warming. Cars, industry, and power stations all give off a greenhouse gas called **carbon dioxide** in their fumes. Coal and natural gas, rice production, and cattle farming create another, called **methane**. Artificial fertilizers and the manufacturing of plastics contribute to the build-up of a third greenhouse gas called **nitrous oxide**.

In hot water

Global warming is heating the oceans. The average temperature of the sea's surface has increased by about 1°F over the last 50 years. As water warms it expands, so the sea has risen 4 inches in that time. If we continue to pump out more greenhouse gases, sea levels could rise by 2 nearly inches every year.

light and heat from Sun

gases in atmosphere

Earth

◀ *Some of the energy that comes to Earth from the Sun is reflected back toward space. As it passes through the atmosphere, gases absorb some of it and give out heat. This is the greenhouse effect.*

▲ *Floods from the sea, such as this one in Dhaka, Bangladesh, make it difficult for people to find clean, fresh water.*

Losing land

Rising seas flood low-lying coasts. Some of the Maldive Islands could disappear under the Indian Ocean within 50 years. Floods in 1998 in Bangladesh caused devastation as the rising sea swamped flat land—and they are likely to do so again. As well as destroying houses and farms, the sea mixes with fresh water, making it salty and unfit to drink.

Meltdown

As global temperatures rise, ice on mountains and around the Poles is melting. If all the ice on Earth were to melt, the sea would rise by about 165 feet. That is not likely to happen, but melting ice will continue to add over half-an-inch to the water level of the oceans every decade.

Working together

In December 1997, representatives from around the world met in Kyoto, Japan to sign an agreement to reduce the production of greenhouse gases. The aim is to cut down fuel consumption and use **alternative energy**. France, Britain, and Germany are now releasing fewer greenhouse gases. **Solar cells** are becoming cheaper, and wind power is generating more of the world's electricity. All 160 countries that signed at Kyoto are working to slow global warming. The world needs them to succeed.

Water in the future

People in richer countries use lots of water, regarding supplies as endless. As more people throughout the world adopt this high consumption, water resources have become stretched.

Water wars

When two countries have to share the same freshwater source, disputes can break out. The River Euphrates provides water for Syria, but rises in Turkey. The Turks are building 20 dams, which are to be completed in 2005, but the Syrians worry that this will stop water reaching their country, drying up their supplies.

Syria has been funding a **guerrilla war** across the border between the two countries. Turkey, in turn, has threatened military action if Syria continues its aggression. Similar battles are occurring all over the world wherever water is scarce.

▼ *If a new dam is built, it will offer these Turkish villagers an improved water supply.*

▲ *Desalination plants, such as this one in Oman, are likely to play a major role in the future of the world's water supplies.*

Salty solution

Nearly all the world's water is in the sea. If this can be made drinkable, no one need be thirsty. Removing salt from seawater is called **desalination**. It can be done, but the processes involved are expensive. The Scilly Isles, off England, rely on only two small aquifers. Water supplies were expected to run out in 1992. But a desalination plant was built, and now people drink converted seawater.

Positive action

In 1992, representatives from around the world met at a big conference in Dublin to begin planning for water in the future. They recognized that clean, fresh water is essential for life and the environment, and decided that it must be looked after. This became part of *Agenda 21*, a plan for all countries to create a better world in the 21st century.

A change of attitude

People are beginning to look at water in a new way. As supplies run dry or become poisoned by pollution, we can no longer take them for granted. Now we are aware of the problems of water in the future, we need to work together to solve them.

Future fresh water

Many other ideas have been tested for improving freshwater supplies. Both California, and the English Channel Island called Jersey have investigated shipping in water by supertanker. America and Israel have experimented with artificial rain. There has even been a suggestion that icebergs could be towed from the Poles to the Middle East.

How you can help

We all need to use water wisely. Whether at home, in our leisure time, or when choosing the products we buy, we can each do a little to improve the state of water in our environment.

Saving supplies

Brushing your teeth with the faucet running wastes about 2 gallons of water every minute. But by rinsing your brush in a mug, you'll use only half-a-pint at a time.

A bath can use more than 25 gallons of water. But a short shower uses only a third of that amount. Dripping faucets can waste 20 pints of water a day, so turn them off tightly.

▲ *This volunteer beach clean-up in Sandy Hook, New Jersey, was organized by a group called "Clean Ocean Action."*

▲ *Leaving the faucet running while you clean your teeth wastes gallons of water every day.*

Flushing the toilet uses a lot of water. Try adjusting the **ball cock**, or filling a plastic bottle with water, sealing it and resting it in the **cistern**. This cuts down the amount of water the toilet uses every time you flush.

A sprinkler in the garden uses over 200 gallons of water an hour. But rain from roofs can be drained into barrels. You can then use it to fill a watering can and water the plants that need it. Growing plants that prefer drier conditions can also save water in the garden.

Cleaning up

Rubbish on beaches, lake shores, and river banks is unpleasant for us, and deadly for wildlife. Around a million birds and 100,000 marine mammals die every year due to plastic litter alone. Metal rings from cans may damage birds. Animals can become tangled in old nets, and plastic bags may trap and kill smaller creatures.

Sometimes groups organize river or coastal clean-ups. If no one is doing this near you, why not start up your own group? People working together can help to improve the environment and care for wildlife and plants.

▼ *Rainwater can be collected from drainpipes into barrels, or water butts, ready to be used in the garden.*

Careful with chemicals

Pouring oil, paint, bleach, and other chemicals down the drain creates problems for water treatment plants. But most local communities have facilities which allow you to dispose of these common pollutants safely.

In stores it is often very difficult to decide which items have been produced at the expense of the environment. But organic food is guaranteed to have been grown without artificial chemicals. You could even try producing your own organic food at home or at school. Plant a patch of vegetables and let them grow without adding chemical sprays or artificial fertilizers.

Getting involved

Some people work full time to help save the world's water. **NGOs** (Non-governmental organizations) tackle problems by spreading information about their cause all around the world, appealing to people for help. Some try to improve lives in poor communities, by setting up safe water supplies. Other groups work for the environment as a whole. NGOs give us all a chance to act. You can help by becoming a member of one, or raising money to send. You'll find some useful addresses on page 44 of this book.

Water projects

Here are four practical ways to find out about water and what it can do.

Hot water fountain

In this project you can watch hot water rising above cold, as it does in the ocean when warm and cold currents meet.

You will need a large, clear glass jar and a clear glass bottle that fits inside the jar. Fill the jar, not quite to the top, with cold water. Tie string around the neck of the small bottle so you can carry it. Fill the small bottle from the hot faucet, add ink or food dye, and lower it into the jar until it sits on the bottom.

The warm, colored water should rise up like a fountain and settle in a layer on the surface of the cold water.

From liquid to frozen

This simple experiment shows how water expands when it freezes into ice.

Fill a plastic sandwich box to the brim with water and press on the lid. Leave it overnight in the freezer. The next day you will find that the frozen water has forced the lid off your box.

This is why bottled drinks are never filled to the cap. If the drink froze, the ice would burst the bottle. Ice can be incredibly powerful. When it forms in mountain cracks, it can split the stone. This helps to wear away the rock.

1 Fill large jar with cold water.

2 Loop string around small bottle of hot, colored water.

3 Dangle bottle inside jar and watch hot water rise.

Water turbine

Running water can be used to drive powerful turbines. This project shows how it works.

You'll need the bottom half of a dishwashing liquid bottle. Carefully make eight holes evenly spaced around the side of the bottle, close to the bottom. Enlarge the holes with a pencil, each time pressing the pencil into the side of the bottle at an angle. All the holes should point in the same direction.

Make two more holes near the top of the half bottle. Tie a short string between them, and attach this to a longer piece of string so you can dangle the turbine under a faucet.

As water from the faucet gushes through the holes, the bottle turbine will spin. Remember not to leave the faucet on for too long, and catch the water in a bowl so that you can use it for something else.

Separating salt

Whatever is dissolved in water will add its flavor. Minerals dissolved from rocks give the sea its salty taste. And when seawater evaporates in the heat of the Sun, it leaves deposits of salt behind.

To see how this happens, pour a table-spoon of salt into a saucer of warm water. Stir until the salt has dissolved. Now leave the saucer on a windowsill or outside in a sheltered position for a day or two. The water will evaporate, leaving behind salt crystals. This works more slowly in cool, wet weather, and quicker when it is hot and dry.

That's why in the warm waters around the equator there is more evaporation and the sea is saltier.

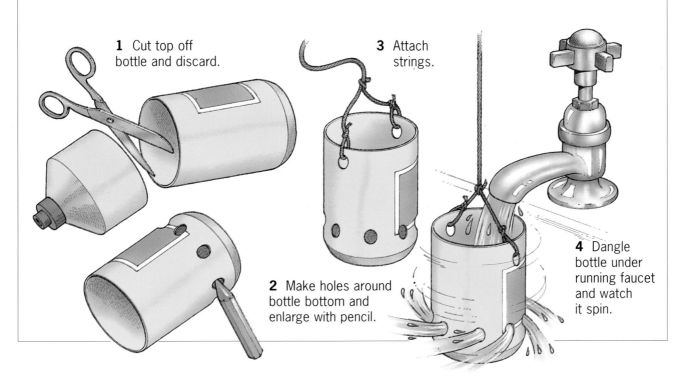

1 Cut top off bottle and discard.

2 Make holes around bottle bottom and enlarge with pencil.

3 Attach strings.

4 Dangle bottle under running faucet and watch it spin.

Water facts and figures

Biggest, deepest, longest, widest, highest...

The Pacific is the world's largest ocean. The Marianas Trench is its deepest point, at 6.8 miles below sea level.

The world's longest river is the Nile in Africa, flowing over 4,168 miles. But the River Amazon in South America carries more water.

Lake Superior in the U.S. has the largest surface area of all lakes. It covers nearly 30,880 square miles.

The longest glacier is the Lambert-Fisher Ice Passage in Antarctica, at 250 miles.

The world's deepest lake is Lake Baikal in Siberia, plunging over a mile at its deepest point. It contains 20 percent of the world's fresh water—more than any other lake.

When rivers flow over cliffs, they can create spectacular waterfalls. The Angel Falls (above) in Venezuela, South America, are the highest in the world, measuring an amazing 3,263 feet. Niagara Falls, on the border between the U.S. and Canada, is tiny in comparison, at only 170 feet high.

Too wet or too dry?

The world's most deadly flood occurred in 1877 when the Hwang-ho River in China burst its banks. Nearly one million people were killed by the destruction it caused.

In July 1993, there was rain for 49 days around the Missouri and Mississippi rivers. In St. Louis, the river rose by 17 feet to the highest level ever recorded. More than 50,000 people had to leave their homes, and 30 died.

In the Atacama Desert, Chile, many years may pass between showers of rain. This is the driest land on Earth.

Swakopmund, in Namibia, Africa, is one of the driest seaside towns, receiving only half-an-inch of rain a year. Most of that water comes from sea mist.

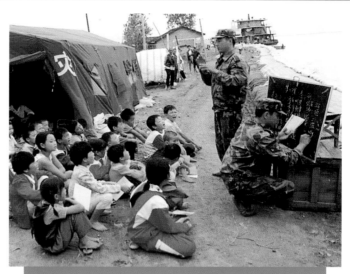

Some of the world's worst flooding occurs along the Yangzte River in China. In 1998, after heavy rains, it rose to its highest recorded level and more than a thousand people were killed. These children are being taught on a **dyke** alongside the river, because their school has been washed away.

Water everyday

Water is heavy. The water in an average bath weighs about a quarter of a ton, and in a swimming pool over 1,100 tons!

Making the paper for one copy of this book used about 6 gallons of water. A pair of shoes takes 8½ gallons, and a bar of chocolate 2 pints.

Natural facts

Your body is an amazing 70 percent water. A cucumber contains 95 percent. Potatoes are 80 percent water, and bread 35 percent. Most meat is about 70 percent water.

Some plants and animals in dry areas go without new water for long lengths of time. The biggest cactus in the world, the saguavo, can store nearly 9 tons in its branches and stem. The Arabian camel can survive with only three-quarters of its natural body fluid.

Water across the globe

Water is not distributed evenly around the world. People use it differently depending on where they live. These maps give you information about water across the globe.

If you compare the map below with the one at the top of the following page, you'll see how Central Africa receives plenty of rain in a year, yet only about half the population has access to safe water. On the other hand, although the Middle East has very low rainfall, this does not deprive most Saudis, Iranians, and Israelis of safe drinking water. But if you look at the third map, you'll see how these richer countries are surrounded by seawater that is particularly badly polluted.

Average annual rainfall

▼ *Rain falls unevenly all over the world. This map shows the average distribution of rainfall throughout the whole year.*

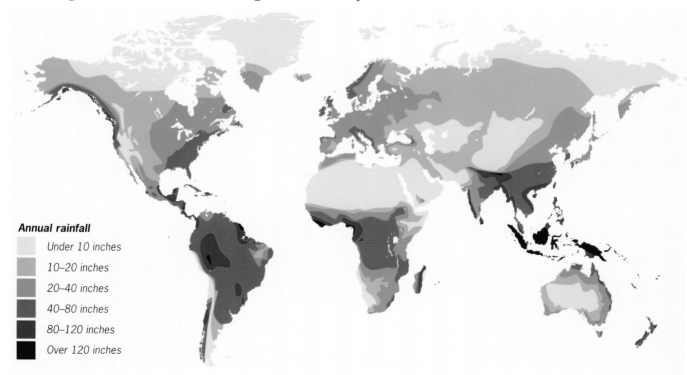

Annual rainfall

- Under 10 inches
- 10–20 inches
- 20–40 inches
- 40–80 inches
- 80–120 inches
- Over 120 inches

Water supply and use

▼ *Not everyone has access to safe drinking water. Some people use—and waste—much more than others.*

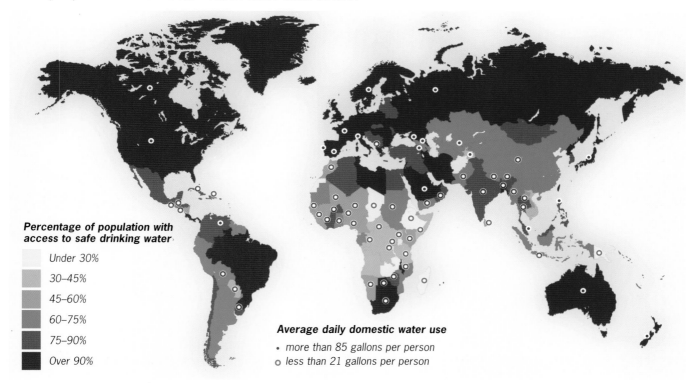

Percentage of population with access to safe drinking water

- Under 30%
- 30–45%
- 45–60%
- 60–75%
- 75–90%
- Over 90%

Average daily domestic water use

- more than 85 gallons per person
- less than 21 gallons per person

Water pollution

▼ *Seas and rivers are polluted all over the world. The worst-affected areas are usually close to big cities and industries.*

Water pollution

- Severely polluted rivers
- Severely polluted seas and lakes
- Less polluted seas and lakes
- Areas of frequent oil pollution by shipping

Further information

Many organizations supply information about various aspects of water in the environment. You can find out more by looking at their websites—or by sending a large, stamped, self-addressed envelope for project news.

WORLDWIDE CONCERN (NGOs)

American Oceans Campaign
600 Pennsylvania Avenue, SE, Suite 210, Washington, D.C., 20003
http://www.americanoceans.org/

Friends of the Earth works for clean rivers and fresh water supplies. A 1999 report *Dam Removal Success Stories* shows how over 465 dams have been removed from U.S. rivers and streams, with ecological benefits.
1025 Vermont Avenue, NW,
Washington, D.C., 20005
http://www.foe.org/

Greenpeace reports environmental damage to the world, aiming to stop further destruction. Greenpeace has a website for young people.
1436 Upper Street, NW,
Washington, D.C., 20009
http://www.greenpeaceusa.org/

National Wildlife Federation takes action on issues including water quality and international wetlands. They produce publications and magazines.
8925 Leesburg Pike, Vienna, Virginia, 22184
http://www.nwf.org/

▲ *Aid agencies set up safe water supplies in many drought-stricken areas of the world. This pump is in Nakaseke, Uganda.*

Oxfam helps people worldwide to improve their lives and care for the environment. They produce educational materials.
26 West Street, Boston, Massachusetts, 02111
http://www.oxfamamerica.org/

WorldWide Fund for Nature (WWF) has a network in 100 countries and works to help animals and plants, including issues affecting water pollution. Their website has a special area for children and schools.
1250 24TH Street , NW, Washington, D.C., 20037-1175
http://www.wwf–uk.org/

WATER IN THE U.S.

Clean Water Action 1320 18ᵀᴴ Street, NW, Washington, D.C., 20036

Renew America identifies and promotes organizations protecting, restoring, and enhancing the environment.
1200 18ᵀᴴ St., NW, Washington, D.C., 20036
http://solstice.crest.org/sustainable/renew_america/

Water Environmental Federation is a non-profit making educational and technical organization of experts that supplies fact sheets.
601 Wythe Street, Alexandria, Virginia, 22314-1994
http://www.wef.org/PublicInfo/index.htm

Water Quality Association 4151 Naperville Road, Lisle, Illinois, 60532

To find out about water near you, contact your local water company.

OTHER USEFUL CONTACTS

For more information about Living Machines (page 15): http://www.livingmachines.com
The Earth Centre, Doncaster, Yorkshire, England

The Amazing Environmental Organizations Web Directory Earth's biggest environmental search engine, can provide details on topics such as *Pollution*, *Water Resources*, *Agriculture,* and *Sustainable Development*
http://www.webdirectory.com/

ECO News (Environmental News Service) P.O. Box 351419, Los Angeles, California, 90035-9119

EnviroLink Network is the largest online environmental information resource
5808 Forbes Avenue, Pittsburgh, Pennsylvania, 15217
http://www.envirolink.org/

▲ *Many organizations also help people such as this girl near Khulna, Bangladesh, when too much water becomes a threat.*

Further reading

Acid Rain by Alex Edmonds (Watts, 1996)

Acting for Nature: What Young People Around the World are Doing to Protect the Environment by Sneed et al (Heyday Books, 2000)

Against the Elements: Water by Hazel Richardson (Watts, 1998)

Drinking Water Quality–Taking Responsibility (Waterworks Publishing, 1998)

Drinking Water: Refreshing Answers to All Your Questions (Texas A & M University Press, 1995)

Energy Forever? Water Power by Ian Graham (Wayland, 1998)

Earth Alert! Coasts by John Baines; *Rivers* by Sheila Whiting (Wayland, 1998)

Our Poisoned Waters by Edward F. Dolan (Cobblehill, 1997)

Glossary

acid rain Rain containing chemicals from smoke, which harms water and forest life.

algal bloom Millions of tiny plants, called algae, which spread over water.

alternative energy Power from unlimited resources, such as wind, Sun, and waves.

aqueduct A man-made channel or pipe that carries water across country.

aquifer Porous underground rocks that take in and store water.

artificial fertilizers Chemicals added to crops to help them grow.

atmosphere The gases surrounding Earth, mostly nitrogen (78%) and oxygen (21%).

bacteria Microscopic living things.

ball cock A device that controls the level of water in a tank.

carbon dioxide A gas in the air that plants need and humans and animals breathe out.

catalytic converter A device that is fitted to a car to lessen pollution from its fumes.

chlorine A chemical used to purify water, making it safer to drink.

cholera A disease spread by dirty water.

cistern A tank for storing water.

condense To turn from vapor to liquid.

currents Large-scale movements of water in a river, lake, or ocean.

dam A wall built across a river to hold back water, raising its level.

desalination Removing salt from seawater to make it drinkable.

dissolve When a solid breaks down into tiny particles, blending into a liquid.

dyke A wall or bank built alongside a river to contain the flow and prevent flooding.

European Union (EU) European countries working together economically and socially.

environmentalists People working to save and protect the environment.

evaporate To turn from liquid to vapor.

fertile Land that is fertile has rich soil that produces good crops.

filter beds Tanks, usually full of stones, through which water passes to be cleaned.

food chain A series of plants and animals, each of which is food for the one after it.

glacier A slow-moving river of ice.

global warming The theory that the Earth is becoming hotter because of air pollution.

greenhouse gases Gases in the atmosphere that trap the Sun's energy, giving off heat.

guerilla war An armed conflict in which small groups of fighters launch surprise attacks and avoid large-scale battles.

heavy metals Dense metals, such as lead and mercury, which harm the environment.

hydrocarbons Gases, such as methane, made up of hydrogen and carbon.

hydroelectricity Power generated by water-driven turbines.

irrigation Providing crops on dry land with water brought from elsewhere.

lock A section of a river or canal where gates can be closed to raise the water level, allowing boats to move upstream.

methane A greenhouse gas produced by rotting plants or manure.

microorganisms Any microscopic living things, such as bacteria.

mineral A material that can be dug out of the Earth, such as salt or diamonds.

monsoon A wind which blows over the Indian Ocean, bringing heavy rain to Southern Asia from April to September.

nitrates Chemicals containing nitrogen that plants need for healthy growth.

nitrous oxide A greenhouse gas that comes from fertilizers and burning coal.

NGOs Groups that work independently of government authorities.

oxygen A gas in the air that all life needs to survive. We take it in when we breathe.

parasite A plant or animal which feeds off another life form by living on or inside it.

pesticide A chemical sprayed on crops to kill insect pests.

plankton Tiny plants and animals in water that provide food for many water creatures.

plague A fast-spreading, often deadly disease. Bubonic plague is carried by fleas living on rats in filthy, unhygienic areas.

pollution Damage to any part of the environment, such as water, land, or air.

porous Has small holes that let liquids in.

radioactive Containing elements that give out energy which is harmful in high doses.

reservoir A store of water, particularly a man-made lake behind a dam.

sedimentary rock Rock made up of layers of mud, sand, etc, laid down by water.

sewage Used water, carrying human waste.

sewer A network of pipes, usually under ground, that carries away sewage.

solar cells Devices which convert light into electricity.

spring A place where water from an aquifer naturally emerges on the Earth's surface.

turbine A rotating device that uses the force of moving water to produce power.

typhoid A disease caused by bacteria living in dirty water.

water cycle The continuous circulation of water from sea to sky and back.

water table The highest level of underground water, such as in an aquifer.

water vapor The gas that water turns into when it evaporates.

wetlands Areas where land is permanently under water, such as marshes and swamps.

Index